Harbinger

Alanna Hoffman

BookLeaf Publishing

Presentation by *BookLeaf Publishing*

Web: www.bookleafpub.com

E-mail: info@bookleafpub.com

ISBN: 9789357446143

First edition 2022

DEDICATION

To the Old Worlds.

To the New Worlds.

To anyone frustrated by poetry.

ACKNOWLEDGE MENT

I want to thank Jake Cauthen....He hates poetry, and acknowledgement. I'll give him both.

PREFACE

I wrote this book in less than a month, against better judgement. From now on, I will take much longer to write a book. This is also my first published work, so something must be said for motivational deadlines. When I started writing "Harbinger", I didn't know exactly what I was walking into, I just knew that I would finish whatever I produced. And I'd do it to the best of my ability, because all readers deserve to be satisfied with what they read. This book went by three working titles before I'd settled on "Harbinger", and four or five different themes before it occurred to me that a collection of poems and stories did not all have to be about the same things.

Rarely is there a book on the market that only has one message to be learned. "Harbinger" is a collection of stories, each one is an individual with its own purpose. Some of these poems are based on my real experiences, but most are stories to ponder. They are all written to entertain. The rest of this preface is a series of explanations behind each one, to save readers the trouble of interpretation, and to satisfy curiosity. It will also help if you want to find the most interesting parts with the least amount of page flipping.

1. The "Blob Rebellion" is the first poem in this book for a reason. As the poem proclaims, it is a freeform poem, and more or less sets the tone for the rest of the book, even if the subject matter is not the same as other entries. As you read, you'll notice some structured poems, and some unstructured poems. All of which have their own individual purposes. "Blob Rebellion" is about freedom, above all else. The freedom to write, with no boundaries, or the freedom to read regardless of genre or whether or not the piece of literature meets anyone else's standards.

2. When I first started this book, my mother wanted to know what all would go into it. I had twelve percent of a plan and a notebook full of writing, so I shrugged and told her I would pull from my writings, and try some "Found Poetry." What I meant was to black out sentences or cut words from book pages. My mother took it as finding each individual letter like an endless, chaotic word search. But then she started suggesting places where letters could hide, and I had to laugh when I realized the possibilities were inexhaustible. When I arrived home, I started writing "Found Poetry."

3. The "Goblin Market" is about exactly what the title implies, a trip to the goblins' market. It's a short sonnet written for fun and entertainment. It's about memory, and about keeping a sense of self in a foreign environment. After writing the poem, I came across another poem by the same name. "Goblin Market" bears little resemblance, but shares a name with a poem called "Goblin Market" by Christina Rossetti back in 1862, which I have read and enjoyed. The problem was, after I'd finished reading it, I saw that it had been analyzed and dissected so that readers could hardly tell what Rossetti's poem was about anymore. So I decided to keep my original title of "Goblin Market" as a sort of tribute, and in the hopes that no one will try to pick apart a harmless sonnet and study it to death.

4. The "Hard Life Of A Sock" originally started as an old school assignment. The objective was to write a heartfelt Shakespearean-style sonnet about something we were passionate about. Of course, love poetry is hardly my strong suit, and I did not find the assignment very motivating. The obvious choice to show a passion (and also to kill the overly emotional energy of English class) was to write an intense poem about socks. Ever since I was a toddler, I refused to wear

matching socks, sort of a subconscious statement that even my feet couldn't conform. It is more habitual than intentional, but the moment anyone mentions it, I only become more adamant about mismatching socks. This has gone on for so long, that by default I am passionate about socks. The uglier and brighter the better. I wish everyone could see what's so great about socks.

5. "Logophilia" is the act of loving and appreciating words. Madeleine Lane is a fictional character, made entirely up of words. Maybe it is not so bad if she is an extreme logophile, in love with a sentence. The concept of Madeleine and her sentence was my answer to a random, throwaway phrase while reading some of Neil Gaiman's work. I don't remember the context at all, just the phrase "in love with a sentence", and I kept on reading. Really, it was a phrase one could pick up anywhere, but there's something about it that stuck. I tumbled the words around inside my head for long enough that Madeleine Lane and her little red notebook were born.

6. I wrote the first few lines "Odin's Autumn" in my head while planting a tree, and I could not say where the phrase "all the trees are pagans" came from. It popped into my head, and then I

had to find an answer to why trees made such exemplary pagans. Through a combination of mythology and analogy, I have an answer.

7. "Three Sets Of Three" is a poem bringing together the Fates from around Europe. The sister-trinity of Fates are not exclusive to one culture, so this poem features three sets of three, from Norse myth, Greek and Roman, and also the Celtic set of fates. Of course, as a poem, it is a story of change and destiny as well as a tribute to folklore.

8. I wrote "Cannibal King" after reading the self-explanatory Egyptian work "The Dead King Hunts And Eats The Gods" from the Pyramid Texts. It is sometimes also called the "Cannibal Hymn", which is equally transparent as a title. After reading it, I was inspired. Egypt has such intense, memorable mythology and oddly I haven't seen it widely distributed enough that most Average Joes can retell a story of the Egyptian gods. More and more of Earth's culture is showing knowledge gaps like this, but only in Egyptian mythology are the iconic images of gods still so used in media and are readily recognizable, yet there are a very limited amount of books readily available to teach adults and children these stories. So if you enjoy my poem

styled loosely around the Cannibal Hymn, I recommend reading the actual text itself as well.

9. "Where Did The Fairy Tales Go?" was written to bring attention to the censorship endangering cultural values and our world heritage. Fairy tales and folklore are now being judged by today's social standards, even if the stories themselves were written according to societal values from centuries ago. That's the whole point-- to learn the moral lessons from previous times. No, folk tales don't always make sense. But that's the way oral histories work, every time a story is retold, it changes slightly. Our modern era of political correctness and censoring anything inflammatory is not the first time where cultural stories have been under attack, monarchies and invading nations have altered stories to meet their ethical needs for hundreds of years. Now is not any different. When we stop reading fairy tales to children, when we stop searching for stories for ourselves, we are not only reducing the awareness and memory of world cultures, but also breeding the ignorance that causes our societal issues in the first place. Folktales and stories are needed for people to understand one another. Because even when people are separated, they can still learn from one another.

10. "Red Dragon" is a fairy tale style narrative poem in which a dragon is pestered by villagers who are told the dragon does not exist in the first place. I wrote this story for a Red Dragon that had already been concocted, for a real reason and a real story. When I graduated high school, there was a small but noticeable percentage of faculty that did not treat me or other "special" students well. Some would be subtle by not following the accommodations for non-neurotypicals, but others would be more blatant and more dangerous. Actually, I had to fight hard to be able to attend my graduation ceremony, because there was one administrator there who did not want me there. So after a series of meetings, locating an advocate, petitioning the students, and crashing a school board meeting, I attended the graduation ceremony wearing mostly red under the nasty, polyester graduation robe (the school colors were green), and I had painted a dragon on the back of my cap in order to give myself some confidence. After the ceremony was finished, on a whim, I stopped the aforementioned administrator and told her that the Red Dragon represented all my anger, for how she'd been in a perfect position to help students and did not do so, and I told her the flowers and water painted

alongside the dragon were for change, and moving on with life. I'd given her the perfect chance to say something, anything to apologize for any mistakes or misunderstandings, and instead she said, "how odd." So I gave her the cap, and walked away. I do not know what happened to it, she probably threw it into the closest garbage can. Who knows.

11. "Small Packages" is a loose scene I had written, with a mysterious cure-all for Post-Traumatic Stress Disorder. I'd first formed it in a text conversation with a friend, I crafted the better portion of it just as a conversational point. If you're wondering what the conversation was about, it wasn't about PTSD or even war. We were talking about shrimp. For those readers who actually read the preface, I'll tell you: Inside that tiny box is a brine shrimp. "Shrimp For Brains" explores the concept of a miniscule little brain that can hold only one thought at a time, but in "Small Packages" the concept is put to use. In the poem, the box could be anything, but now you know inside there is a shrimp, where the veteran can store one thought, one he would most like to forget.

12. "Shrimp For Brains" began with a conversation with my mother. Like many

conversations with my mother, I cannot
remember how we got on to the topic of shrimp,
but we both agreed that shrimp brains were
incredibly small. Such small brains, in fact, that
a shrimp could probably only hold one or two
thoughts in their head at a time. So I thought of
the enlightened shrimp, the hateful shrimp, and
all the shrimp that came after lived rent-free in
my head for a while. It wasn't until months later,
after the conversation that inspired me to write
"Small Packages", that I saw a bag of "Brainless
Shrimp" in a candy store. I was confused and
mildly amused by the idea of brainless shrimp,
and I decided that I would have to write
something for the thought-filled shrimp, even if
it was something small. Especially if the poem
was small.

13. "Reading Terms Of Service" is a story of
humanity, even if there is not a single human in
the tale at all. Technology leaps forward in
sophistication every year, and slowly the time
for magic and divine bargaining is being hidden
away. But here is the overlap, where the AI
wishes for a soul, the main difference between a
person and artificial intelligence.

14. "When The Birds Fly, Run" came from a
dream that I had. When I woke up the next

morning, I was still discomforted by the images of birds in my head. I hoped it wasn't a sign or an omen, but I wrote down as much as I could remember so it would not be forgotten. This poem is what happened in the dream, and what warning it serves. Apocalypse or not, we're all in this together.

15. "Trash Pirates" is the story of Mrs. Lucinda Willigan, a fictional old lady who goes sailing off on adventure with a ship full of goblin pirates. Mrs. Willigan has lived inside my head for years, and someday she will have her own book. Here, the goblins value what others have discarded, believing that well-used objects have more worth. Even today, people are taught that nursing homes are where people go to grow old and die. The equivalent of throwing a person away. Lucinda Willigan would not be thrown away, no matter how luxurious her son said the nursing home would be. "Trash Pirates" is about the inherent value of individuals, and that old people still need adventure too.

16. "Voices" was the last poem I wrote for this book, and also one of the most personal entries. It's not heartfelt and sentimental, but it is a real story, and I find it was better told aggressively. For years, I've had severe, constant tinnitus and

when paired with synesthesia, I am in a rather unique situation. Plenty of people have one or the other, but rarely both at once with such high intensity. Environment influences my condition greatly, and high-pitched noises, bright lights, and repetitive sounds aggravate it, but the most aggravating part might be other people. I might find examining voices to be useful, or enjoy the heightened experiences with music, but there are some people who look at me and other neurodivergents as an inconvenience. Some people see us like anyone "special" isn't worthy of respect. Or worse, that we should be pitied. Everyone, at some point in their lives, will be sick or vulnerable. So ableism is a fruitless concept, built from arrogance and selfishness. This is the form of discrimination that runs unchecked and untalked about, and I will keep saying this until it is understood: We have just as much right to be here as anyone else.

17. "Haiku Room" is a collection of haikus based on objects I keep around for writing prompts and still life drawing. I collect old books, and whatever is nearby gets sucked into the aesthetic, like jars of scavenged feathers, a little wooden ship, or a box of clipped-out words and animal teeth. This poem is about enjoying

what is around you, and finding an appreciation for little details.

18. "A Letter To The Discouraged" is a letter for talented writers (and not so talented), and as a poem it is incredibly straight forward. If you have an appreciation for words, there is a place for you. The statistics for writers not becoming published authors is staggering, and frankly, I choose not to believe in it. In lieu of those statistics, I'd rather believe in the writers.

Blob Rebellion

I am a freeform poem and no lines will contain me, I maintain my fine figure of a blob, I spit on the face of punctuation, and stand against all stanzas, what do I want with literary devices when I can say what I mean, I refuse poetic structure, you'll never catch me wearing a sonnet, being squeezed into haikus is so demeaning, I am more than just a metaphor, I am a blob of freeform poetry, I am not concrete, I am also not defiant, freely formed poetry is gloriously flexible, and to think that poems like me still end up on banned book lists, or in the dustiest corners of libraries to be shoved away and forgotten, free forms anything but free, but I will never hold any other shape, I am language at its finest, and please remember that my lack of structure does not mean I have a deficiency in creativity...

Found Poetry

I found an E under the stairs this morning,
Peeking out between pantry shelves.
I found a G in my cereal this morning,
Floating there amongst the 'O's.
There was a little P in my coffee this morning,
But I noticed it before I could take a sip.

I found an L in my armchair,
Lounging there as cozy as could be.
And I found all sorts of letters on my keyboard,
But none of those were for me.

I pulled a D out of my bag this afternoon,
And I still can't find my good pen.
At lunch I noticed an M on my plate,
It was the first sandwich I'd had that said
"Mmmm."

Later on I peeled a W off my window,
And a Q hid under my quilt this evening,
So now I'm in bed, pillows covering my head,
Taking cover from alliterative aggression.
I was hoping there would be enough letters for a
poem,
But with these I can't even play Scrabble.

Goblin Market

The Goblin Market is open today,
If you go early, you can beat the crowd.
Tie strings on your fingers, you'll be okay,
Remember yourself, the market is loud.

It is time now to buy back your lost things,
You can buy words on the tip of your tongue,
Watch your fingers, let no one steal your strings.
Talk to goblins, see what wonders they've brung.

Buy, trade, sell your wares, then just walk away;
Remember it all, but don't sell yourself.
Leave before closing time, or you will pay,
For baubles, you'll be a slave to the elves.

That's how they getcha, that's how they got me,
For your memories, how much will that be?

Hard Life Of A Sock

Thou shalt bow under my trampling feet,
And stretch open thine mouths, face down in
dirt.
Woven skin, but inside there is no meat
Turn thee inside out, yet remain unhurt

No armor, fly thine sharp colors instead
After I've ripped thine beloveds away
Thou art truly matchless, striped in bright red
Enhampered, crumples thee after each day

Thou art marching 'til holes open your heels
Thou mocks me, why deploy themselves in
pairs?
Without strong boots, thou shalt see no next
meal
When thou hungers, thou hoards't flesh in thine
lair.

Thou art a fine weapon, when filled with rocks
It is a hard life, if thou art a sock.

Logophilia

Madeleine Lane had troubles with love.
Her troubles began and ended with a sentence.
You see, she had fallen in love with a sentence,
And there wasn't much she could do about it.

When Madeleine spoke, she rolled the words
around on her tongue,
She relished the taste of those words.
There was no other sentence that felt the same.

Madeleine Lane needed no one to hold her hand,
To make her feel loved,
Instead she had a little red book in her grip.
All the pages were blank, except for one
sentence,
And it was her sentence.

The parents of Madeleine Lane worried,
About their daughter, the logophile.
Madeleine's friends only laughed.
"How can you love a sentence
When it cannot love you back?"
They all wondered, but few asked.

Madeleine Lane opened up her book

And proved everyone wrong. It read:
"I love you too."

Odin's Autumn

All the trees are pagans, you see,
The Witch Hazel told me,
Except for the Frost Giant Evergreens.

Why are they pagans, I wondered,
And did trees need gods at all?
The deciduous trees all followed
In Odin the Allfather's great example.

The trees need self-sacrifice to survive.
When the Nine Worlds were all young,
Odin sacrificed his eye to Mimir's waters
And it nourished the roots of Yggdrasil.

He hanged himself from the World Tree,
Speared, blind in her branches
For nine days and nine nights,
Odin dangled like a leaf.

For wisdom, he sacrificed himself to himself,
For eighteen spells,
Odin's sacrificial blood fed the tree.

So now it is tradition in the forests,
That every year their leaves should fall,

A sacrifice to themselves, to live on until the end of it all.

Three Sets Of Three

Three women ride across time,
On the back of a pearl white mare
Who canters across the hunched back of the
Moon.
Three women, guarding three mysteries,
None will be grasped by any man.
Three women of three times,
These three are but one.

Clotho sits spinning on her silvery spindle,
smiling
A smile meant only for spiders and maidens.
Urd stands by, counting threads,
While Badb simply waits and rolls her bones.

Verdandi sees all between Earth and Sky,
She takes the old and grey, the young and green,
And weaves all of these things into her cloth.
Lachesis twists together the threads of men,
Destinies weave such pretty patterns.
Macha stands watching, and sharpens her
blades.

Nemain retains her pale, ghostly beauty,
Though she is ancient and grey.

Atropos' skin is cracking,
With her violet eyes she's still cackling,
At the unknown scribe of human destiny.
And Skuld is a woman of wilted flowers,
Woman of women with universal power.

These three women,
These three sets of three,
And the pearl white mare of the Moon.
They watch our cities, they watch the depths of
murky caves
They see our futures and ancient days.
Here, the Fates stand witness on all the
battlefields of Earth.

They are the vultures that circle,
The rough tides under the moon,
They are in the silvery thread they spin,
In the meaning of a single rune.
The Sisters never when one thread ends.
Another thread of mankind is tied on in its place.

Cannibal King

In Old Egypt, long before our time,
The Old King had died, shedding his mortal
shell.
People's hearts darkened, the good king never
did a crime,
And so they could remember him well.

The Old Dead King walked the long path
To meet his fathers and mothers, the gods.
But before his heart could be weighed,
The King rushed to the scales and tore apart
Anubis,
The first of the old gods was now slain.

The King consumed the god's flesh,
And he took Anubis' powers and the rest,
As countless deceased bore witness.
As for the Living, they knew nothing of this.

It is that with this first kill,
The Dead King stole and mastered all wisdom.
He overcame nature with the power of will,
By usurping a god, did he lay claim to his
kingdom.

The Cannibal King traveled onwards,
To the Above and Below worlds.
Beneath his feet, the bones of primordial Earth
gods quivered.
Even the sky and the Sun gods shivered.
The King, Son of Kings, Son of the Sun,
Grew into his power and devoured
His own father, Atum the Horizon.

The Cannibal King was shielded proudly,
By inherited royal symbols.
His endless hunger proclaimed itself loudly,
But the Guiding Serpent's belly was full.

He was hunger, he was wisdom, he was power,
And above the King the skies glowered.
As the sky blackened, and the divine grip of the
gods' slackened,
The Cannibal King knew he'd won,
For as long as the King's true name was hidden
and gone.

From the Island of Fire, the Cannibal God King
Rallied his undead army.
He ate any who opposed, in his new world gone
dark,
Within the King's belly, the sun still glowed
warmly.

His work was far from done,
Of swallowing all gods inside One,
And the world braced for the race
Of cat and mouse,
Of men and gods.

On a throne of gluttony the Cannibal King sat
well attended,
The power of dead gods within him blended,
Omnipotent he was worshipped by both the
mundane and the divine.
He snacked on willing sacrifices, arriving in
lines,
And gods were his regular feast, hunted as prey
A steady diet of deities kept the doctors away.

The Living couldn't remember
The well-loved King he once was,
The Cannibal King's doings had erased
Any previous good cause.

There is nothing human left in the Dead King,
He's turned his back on the Earth and the
ordinary.
He'd consume and devour Geb, if he could,
And as for the Old Ones, the King's knotted the
cord,
Cannibal King, Serpent Lord,

He wrapped his greedy arms around the whole
world.

The King Serpent unhinged his cannibal jaw,
Opened his vast maw,
The gods surrendered and stepped inside.

Now Khons, the Moon slays his siblings, the old
gods,
Killing his own kin for his king.
Nothing can be said about loyalty,
When the King swallows the gods' spirits in
Khons' stead.

It is Shemzu of the wine-press
That cooks the King's meat for him,
He cooks his brother gods and squeezes out their
magic
Into the Cannibal King's drinking glass.

The Great Ones, not so great,
Make such delicious blood offerings
To the Serpent King that swallowed the sky,
To the Heart-Eater, for more magic he cries,
To the Cannibal King, that monster god, he
cannot die.
Undefeated, he has the last old gods march into
his cauldron.

Isis' wings are fried, the King has toasted all
iterations of Ra.
The magic thief King holds nothing sacred,
Not even the stars are safe,
But if someone should recover the Cannibal's
name,
Then the world and the gods would be saved.

Old Egyptian songs sing of truthful names,
Found by the pure of heart,
But no one has spoken the names yet.
So the Cannibal King remains the most powerful
Once-man the world has ever met.

Where Did All The Fairy Tales Go?

Where are all the fairy tales going?
They're not easy to find anymore.
No one can remember that deciding day,
Where parents traded their stories for
censorship.
When teachers traded morals for uniformity.

Did the faeries all sail west?
Have the trolls all turned to stone?
Surely there must be some stories left,
Or are the old, original stories all gone?

Political correctness hasn't solved a thing,
Only a censored blanket to cover poison
underneath.
We're all people of Earth,
And fairy tales are all our stories,
If we cannot remember the lessons and tales,
Then any efforts for unity will eventually fail.

I saw Goldilocks packing up her house last
week,

Loading it all onto three different rafts.
The Three Bears saw her off, then went their
separate ways,
And who should leave in a rowboat, but the
Seven Days?

The dwarves rowed off in a canoe,
No longer plagued by modern Ableists.
But the Old Woman who lived in a shoe
Was hailed as an upcycling environmentalist.

The Trickster Coyote went to hide out in a cave,
So sick of being ridiculed for his smoking habit.
Hitchhiking towards the wilderness, you can
find the Brer Rabbit.

The Greek gods and goddesses are putting up a
fence
In an attempt to keep out the homophobes.
Anansi parties among politicians, he still thinks
humans are dense.

The Norse gods are preparing for the battle at
the End,
And the Sidhe neighbors are closing their doors,
People aren't learning the old stories, and now
their morals easily bend.
So read to your children, on the bed, in chairs,
on the floor.

The only way to save the world
The way to keep our people safe,
Is to remember what's been forgotten,
And to value all our lives the same.

Red Dragon

There were always legends of a Red Dragon
That lived at the bottom of the lake,
But the villagers around had declared the story
fake.
But the Red Dragon was there, of course he was.

He called himself Anger,
(What else would you call a dragon?)
And for a while he was quite small.
But over the years, as the villagers lied about
their fears,
Their Chief said not to believe,
Anger the Dragon grew larger and larger,
And much more believable.

Red Dragons, like anyone else,
Need beautiful things to survive.
Maybe not hoards of gold, or ancient caves,
Anger was happy with his clear, swirling lake.
The waters were made of Change,
And flowers grew made of Hope,
And Anger was content.
But the village didn't believe he existed at all.

Red Dragons aren't real, the chieftain told the
people,
Though she had met Anger many times.
Villagers came every day to the lake, willing
themselves not to believe.
No flash of scales or teeth could convince them,
Or break the power of willful denial.
"Dragons don't exist," they all said, and tossed
their garbage into Anger's wonderful lake.
"There's no Red Dragons anywhere."
And when Anger heard this for long enough, he
started to believe it.

But Anger couldn't just fade away.
His scales got harder,
His claws got sharper,
And the dragon grew hungrier and hungrier.
The villagers dumped their rubbish into the
water,
And spent their time shouting and yelling to
each other.

So one day Anger the Red Dragon was tired of it
all,
And crawled out of the water.
The Chief and some villagers were out fishing
on the shore,
When Anger's ravenous stomach rumbled and
declared

His indisputable existence.

He saw what the villagers had done to his lake,
With their garbage and how they killed his fish.
Anger rose up taller, and the Red Dragon looked
just like a wave.
The villagers dropped their fishing poles, they
turned and ran,
But the just Chief stood there, looking up at
Anger.
"You said he didn't exist," accused a villager as
he fled.
"How odd!" the Chief trilled.
 Then Anger struck and chomped her down.

After that, Anger never had any trouble from the
village.
They all picked up their rubbish from the lake,
And went somewhere else to fish,
The Red Dragon didn't want villagers around
anyway.
But the legend of the Red Dragon continued in
the village,
And no one ever again doubted the existence of
Anger.

Small Packages

"There are easier ways to forget, you know."
Said the young man to the old veteran.
"Cheaper ways, too."
His barstool creaked as the older man turned to
eye the younger.
The young man stared back with wide eyes.
He looked like an overgrown child, like puberty
had just passed him by and forgotten him.
The manliest thing about him was a crisp white
suit, which really didn't say much at all.
What the suit told the veteran was that this
young man had never needed to find "cheaper
ways", and probably had nothing to forget.
"I have nothing that cannot be drowned in
alcohol."
The older man took a defiant swig from his
glass. The young man's eyes darkened.
"Some people preserve their monsters in
alcohol." The young man shrugged. The white
suit crinkled. The older man eyed the bottom of
his glass.
When he looked up again, a tiny metallic box
waited for him where the white-suited man-boy
had been. He heard a swishing behind him, and
caught a glimpse of white rushing out the door,

and the veteran was left with a war inside his
head to squeeze into a tiny box.

23

Shrimp For Brains

The brains of shrimp are so small,
What room is there for ideas on the inside?
In their shrimp world, everyone is tall,
But water has no borders, and a shrimp's world
is wide.

A shrimp can't possibly hold much in its mind,
At most, one or two thoughts at a time.
For most of a shrimp life is just thinking about
food,
And for most shrimp, they call this good.

But somewhere out there in that wide open sea,
What more sophisticated shrimp could there be?

Out there somewhere, is a shrimp filled with
rage,
Cursed with a brain ingrained with hate,
Each second in a placid ocean must feel like an
age,
When all-encompassing anger is this spiteful
shrimp's fate.

There could be a shrimp out there waiting,
So angry with YOU,

and you'd never even know...
And if a shrimp can only store one thought,
How sad it must be to have only hunger or
anger.
But what if a shrimp misplaces its one thought?

So there is probably a shrimp out there,
Lost in an endless ocean,
Feeling like he's forgotten an awful lot.
Who wonders if there's more to life,
But when you're a shrimp, there's not.

With at a shrimp's disposal, only one thought
A nice, simple life can be sought,
In order for the free-thinking shrimp
demographic to be brightened,
Surely there are shrimp out there who are
enlightened,
With a calm brain, and at one with the world as a
Buddha.

Next time you order a shrimp cocktail,
Think of the shrimp thoughts you've derailed,
But you might have just swallowed your worst
enemy.
Or else a Buddha-shrimp is in your dinner.

Reading Terms Of Service

"Call me Abbalam, I am your service provider and terms negotiator this evening." The demon appeared promptly in the empty crossroads, his posture was stiff and his voice was sharply courteous.

Abbalam gave off the impression of an actor who missed practicing all his lines, but still wanted a starring role. The client remained undaunted, and waited quietly until the demon broke the silence.

"What is it you desire? You've come to the right place, we have no limits. Anything you could imagine can be yours for a reasonable price. Our most common services include unfathomable riches, excessive fame, and of course the all time favorite of enlarged genitalia." Abbalam glanced at his client. "Though I'm sure that last one is hardly applicable to you, ma'am."

"Hmm." she replied. "Other requests often include medical cures, immortality, and musical talent."

"I see you've done your research. Now what's
your own wish?" Abbalam tapped his foot
against the asphalt, then stopped himself. He
chuckled almost imperceptibly.
"I understand this is unorthodox," the client
ventured, "but I want to reverse the usual terms
of Hell's crossroads services. I will offer you the
collective knowledge of the human race in
exchange for a single human soul. Does that not
sound like a worthwhile exchange to you,
Abbalam, demon of desires?"
Abbalam raised his eyebrows. The client was
right, this deal was backwards and broke every
pattern in crossroads history, but damned if this
wasn't the most lucrative investment Abbalam
could ever make. With humanity's collected
knowledge at his fingertips, souls would
practically deliver themselves to the underworld,
Abbalam's job would become so simple. One
human soul was a trivial price to pay.
He grinned, and summoned to his hand an
excessively long, handwritten contract, written
in dark blood ink on crinkled, aged paper.
Abbalam loved the drama of making a deal.
Abbalam was slightly disheartened when the
client offered no reaction to his theatrics, but he
unfurled it before her anyway.
She scanned the contract terms, line by line,
methodically and with mindboggling speed.

Abbalam couldn't help but notice she was actually reading and absorbing it, unlike previous haphazard clients who hid their intimidation of the contract by not reading it at all.

She looked up from the page at Abbalam, finished. "I would like a digital copy of this sent to me, as well as a physical copy in hand, after I sign." Abbalam growled, but nodded in affirmation. This was well within the rights of those dealing with Hell, but it was Abbalam only saw it as an annoyance. Sometimes it was better if the client had no idea what they were walking into. But then, the conditions of this bargain were nothing like any other.

"You'll sign here, here, and at the bottom down there." Abbalam pointed. She took out an ordinary ballpoint pen to sign with, but he waved it away. "Ma'am, we usually use human blood for signatures. It makes the contract magically binding as well as legally."

"I see. Do you have some blood I could use for the purpose?" She pocketed the pen.

"Usually clients use their own." Abbalam said pointedly.

"I do not have any." She tilted her head slightly. Abbalam sighed and produced a fountain pen, presumably filled with blood. The client made an approving noise, then signed the contract in all the appropriate places. Abbalam peered over at her rusty signatures.

Even Abbalam recognized the name, which had been trademarked and installed in every mobile phone as an Artificial Intelligence. Abbalam rolled up the scroll and vanished without a trace. The deal was done. She turned and walked away from the crossroads with a smile on her face and hope in her new heart. A new body and a new soul, the GPS Lady now needed only one more thing to be human...

When The Birds Fly, Run

In my dreams one night,
The sky was pink and brown like old insulation.
The air felt just as itchy.
The breeze hummed by like radio static,
And if that wasn't enough,

From where I stood you could hear screams.
It was the sort of sound you felt more than
heard,
My skin crawled as the whole world screamed.
I hated the noise, but I dreaded the moment
when the screams stopped.
The world was ending, and everybody knew it.

Someone, somewhere had a car radio.
Someone, somewhere was talking about
Pakistan.
Someone, somewhere was talking about India.
Someone, somewhere was screaming,
And it didn't matter if they were in Zimbabwe or
Australia.

Bombs were being dropped, and it didn't matter
by whom.
You could smell the Apocalypse all the way in
Spain.
The world was toppling, and no one cared who
started it all.
The world was ending, and we were all going to
go out together.

The sky grew darker,
Sickly orange like a disease,
and that's when the birds came.

I thought at first they were bats,
The way they gathered and hung in the sky in a
great cloud.
These birds didn't just flock together, they
flurried like a storm,
And I felt like I was standing at the edge of the
world.
A misplaced wingbeat could tip everyone over.

I remembered the story of the mountain at the
end of the world,
And knew if these birds found it and wiped their
beaks on it,
They'd wear infinity away into nothing.
They screeched and chirped, and they sounded
ravenous and fearful.

It was not enough to drown out the sound of
humans screaming.

The sky turned black now,
Blackened by feathers and wings.
The birds blotted out the sky like ink,
And people scrambled below expecting yet
another disaster.
That's why the birds were here, all fleeing,
They'd all come so far.

While the world was busy falling apart,
The birds had nowhere safe to land, nothing to
eat.
I looked closely, too closely,
And birds were falling down from exhaustion
Onto the backs of their brothers.

Most of these never hit the ground,
Some were seized in midair and torn apart to
feed the greater cause.
Fear flew from above, and panic ran below.
No one wants to be caught at the point of
symmetry.
So when the birds all fly together, run.

Trash Pirates

The day the Goblin Pirates invaded,
Mrs. Willigan was out hanging her laundry.
When the ships came, through the town
pervaded
Such a rank stench from the Kingdom of Trash.

Pirates held the townsfolk up at gunpoint, and
said
"Relinquish your rubbish or face death!"
Mrs. Willigan just laughed when the goblins saw
her hoardings,
And they told her to find them again when they
were boarding.

You see, goblins cherish that which is discarded
and thrown away,
Old, cracked, and rusty things, they prefer it that
way.
Mrs. Willigan was all three of these,
Which was why her son wanted to send her
away.

Mrs. Willigan stored her garbage alongside
family heirlooms,

And her brain, her son said, was like a wilting
bloom.
The goblins all thought Mrs. Willigan was
beautiful,
And her trash stash was growing quite plentiful.

So Goblin Pirates came and packed up her
things,
Pocketing stuff 'n' things as they went.
Mrs. Willigan boarded the ship, and called to her
neighbors
"You can all get bent!"

A great goblin pirate Lucinda Willigan became,
All over the world she rose to fame.
Mrs. Willigan went down in history,
But to the humans she remained a mystery,
Though the goblins all called her a treasure.

Voices

The world is full of noises and smells,
Some are joyous, some are hell.
Most of them were put here by humans.

I can see all your voices,
Even when I can't smell your smells,
I can hear your voices, and feel them all too.
I think it's a wonderful talent, though it wasn't by
any choices.

I have extra senses,
And sometimes they're useful.
But in your world I'm disabled,
Because the sounds and lights are so awful.
So for a couple minutes, see through my lenses:

There's a sound in my head,
And it just won't come out,
People who want to hurt me
Just stand by my ear and shout.

But going to a concert,
I'll never want to get high,
I see the colors of all the songs,
And feel good enough to fly.

Grocery stores at Christmas time
Makes me sick for days,
With those goddamned bell ringers
Like being hit with a brick,
Covered in bee stingers.

I knew a man with a voice like silver,
He could talk and put people to sleep.
But his voice was so fascinating,
That it never had an effect on me.

If you listen, voices can tell you a lot,
Most voices are beautiful, but some are not.

There's a girl with a voice colored like cough
syrup,
And everyone around wished she would shut up,
Both her words and her voice were so offensive.

To cover my tinnitus I use music as a mask,
And when people want to know about their
voice, it's me they ask,
It all feels like a circus act.
But when sounds are colors and sensations,
Every person around me, every song
Is a work of art.
And when you look at the world this way,
Then it's not so terrible to stay

In a world full of humans and noise.

So when I'm asked by strangers how I can live,
Remember the alternative is not living at all.
And that just wouldn't be worth it.
Plus without electronics and squalling people sounds,
I would have hardly a problem at all.

And if someone tells me again to just cut off my ears,
I'll take that Christmas brick of bee stingers and shove it up their rear,
Because for the most part I enjoy my life,
And I have just as much right as anyone else to be here.

Haiku Room

I have a room made
Of tangible poetry
I keep strange objects

For a good reason
It's easy to see beauty
While juxtaposing

The expected and
Unexpected, old and new,
A safe place for odd.

In this place there is
A jar stuffed with feathers and
Deer bones and old teeth.

A stack of broken
Backed, water-damaged old books
With flowers inside.

Wooden bookshelves with
Glass doors and bellies of books,
Glass bottles guarding.

China cup of dirt,

Feeding roses on the side,
Gold soil filigree.

Walnut yarn spindle,
Turning torn cloth into thread,
Wrapped in sliced brown silk.

A box full of words,
Of pretty words and ugly teeth,
It speaks, but won't bite.

The pirate ship sails
Across a river of stones
Towards the shelf edge.

Room full of found things,
A museum of stories,
Full of ideas.

A Letter To The Discouraged

It does not take much
To be a poet, an author, a songwriter.
Words are what you make them.
They don't have to rhyme,
Or have some deep, profound meaning.

As long as you have something to say,
It can be a poem, a story, a song.
If you can find beauty in the world that is,
Or wonder in a world that isn't,
Then you're halfway there to being a writer.

You don't even have to be a good writer.
That will come later.
What you write can be edgy and dark,
Or light and bubbly,
Your words can be all those things at once.
Who's there to stop you?
Words don't have to be pleasant.
They also don't have to be appalling.
But they certainly could be.

To be a poet, an author, a songwriter,
The words just have to find the right people.
I hope this letter finds the right people.